TO BE A WOMAN IN AMERICA 1850-1930

1

TO BE A WOMAN IN AMERICA 1850-1930

ANNETTE K. BAXTER

WITH CONSTANCE JACOBS

Published by **TIMES BOOKS,** a division
of Quadrangle/The New York Times Book Co., Inc.
Three Park Avenue, New York, N.Y. 10016

Published simultaneously in Canada by
Fitzhenry & Whiteside, Ltd., Toronto.

Library of Congress Cataloging in Publication Data

Baxter, Annette Kar.
   To be a woman in America, 1850–1930.

   1. Photography of women. 2. Women—Portraits.
3. United States—Biography—Portraits. I.
I. Jacobs, Constance, joint author. II. Title.
TR681.W6B38   1978   779′.24′0973   78–53299
ISBN 0–8129–0764–7
ISBN 0–8129–6306–7 pbk.

Manufactured in the United States of America.

Designed by Barbara Shapokas

DEDICATION

This book is dedicated to all the women in it, young and old, who let themselves be photographed without suspecting that they were contributing to a larger understanding of our lives as well as their own.

CONTENTS

Photohistorian's Preface

The photographs in this book are the product of a unique photo-research project, a trip of over 5,000 miles in which I crisscrossed the United States, working at 50 major historical sources, museums, universities, and historical societies. Traditionally, photographs from historical societies have been donations from people cleaning out their attics (or those of relatives), but in the past six years, as interest is growing, societies are increasingly able to raise the funds needed to purchase major collections and valuable photographs. I myself have been rummaging for years through the barrels of stereocards to be found in antique shops across the country—and the lighthearted stereoviews represented here were gathered in just that informal way.

The photographs in this book begin with the first common use of paper prints. In this era of early cameras and slow film there was a practical need for the subject to hold still and stare at the black box. Having one's picture taken was an event which occurred once or twice in a lifetime; there was little thought of capturing the quality of everyday life. But as an endless stream of nameless faces and lost stories passed before my eyes, I sought out and selected that tiny percentage of the images which were more candid action shots that showed life as it really was.

Who were the unknown photographers? In this period of primitive equipment, they were professionals, certainly, but a breed of professionals not content to confine themselves to the customary posed portrait, a special kind of photographer with an urge to record.

And record they did. As the camera lens clicked, the moment was preserved forever—and this collection of moments yields a telling picture of American womanhood.

—Constance Jacobs, 1978

Introduction:A Kaleidoscopic History

Like our memories, photographers usually record the static: the family on the front porch, the pets at sleep, the mountain in the distance. Women especially, in our photographic record of them, have so frequently been stalled in their activities by the camera that one is tempted to conjecture that the photographer, usually male, may have preferred the female in non-action. Moving, she might be a disquieting reminder of how much of significance in man's environment is a result of her motion.

The photographs in this volume have been selected in an effort to redress that historical flaw: They are often of women in the act of doing something. Whether marching in a suffrage parade, operating a lathe, prospecting in the Klondike, or feeding her family, the female subject suggests an intensity that transcends our hidden expectations of female behavior. Even in their most conventional guise, as housewives and mothers, teachers and nurses, the women you will observe in these pages appear to have chosen their roles and assumed their tasks with an inveterate purposefulness. If they were silently chafing at the restrictions society imposed upon them or yearning for the opportunities from which they were excluded, you will find little hint of animosity or frustration in their faces.

Their individual identities for the most part unrecorded, they confront us in a profusion of selves: farmers and belles-of-the-ball; immigrants and blacks; athletes and flirts; homebodies and hellions. Clearly they are all Americans, and are all putting a characteristically American stamp upon their experience. The dilemma of their collective future as a sex seems not to be troubling them, even in their moments of militancy. Their faces proclaim that they are at one with themselves in the life of action.

This composite portrait of American women is the fruit of a long search in archives and collections that are little known and have been little used. Unlike most nineteenth-century photographs, those included here usually lack the posed quality called for by slow film and the portentousness of occasions to be memorialized by the camera. Because of their spontaneity, the moods registered in these faces are the universal ones: curiosity and reflection, concentration and abandon, hope and resignation, joy and despair. They are projections of personality and statements of will. They invite us to observe a whole half of humanity whose history has traditionally been portrayed as marginal; who lived, we are told, on the sidelines of life. Through the unchauvinistic eye of the camera, they give the lie to such simplifications.

The complex truth of women's lives is perhaps more accurately approached through the loosely thematic, deliberately kaleidoscopic arrangements observed in these pages than in strict fidelity to chronology. For women have not experienced a logical, systematic progression toward selfhood.

All along their experience has been one of shifting goals and reversals of status. In the seventeenth and eighteenth centuries they enjoyed an esteem which was the consequence of their scarcity and of the active role they played in the economy of the colonies. Nevertheless, an obvious analogy could be drawn between the paternalistic oppression of the British and the patriarchal dominance of husbands. For the most part women accepted their inexorable subordination to male interests and values, though occasionally individuals with the spunk of an Abigail Adams protested the uniformly masculine standards governing their lives.

In the early national period women did assume a novel importance as mentors of the young, molding future citizens of the new democratic nation. But as such, they lost part of their value as persons contributing skill and talent in their own right and entitled to more than the vicarious fulfillments of motherhood. Thus, American women gained no real advance in status during the first two centuries of their history.

Their situation did not improve with the coming of industry. Rapid technological changes and the shift to the factory as the center of production meant that women no longer enjoyed the psychological rewards of home industry, though spinning and weaving, along with other womanly skills recorded in these photographs, sometimes survived in rural areas. The earlier direct relationship of women to the economy was progressively being severed. Even the forceful role they had played in the educational lives of their children in the days of the nascent republic was being preempted by the newly emerging academies and young ladies' seminaries.

With the advent of a full-scale philosophy of domesticity in the mid-nineteenth century, women achieved unprecedented status in one sense as presiding angels of the family circle. Cloistered in the protective setting of the home and enjoined by society from working outside it, middle-class women, especially, created private worlds of their own. Often their world was overwhelmingly religious. Elizabeth Stuart Phelps, author of the best-selling allegorical novel, *The Gates Ajar*, applied the philosophy of the fireside to the heavenly sphere. One of her characters comments: "A happy home is the happiest thing in the world. I do not see why it should not be in any world. I do not believe that all the little tendernesses of family ties are thrown by and lost with this life."

But while it glorified the idea of the home-centered woman, faith also challenged it. Indeed, faith worked hand in hand with the practical impulse toward reform in the larger worlds of abolition, social welfare, and even feminism. In 1868, the same year that *The Gates Ajar* appeared, Mary Abigail Dodge, who wrote under the pen name of Gail Hamilton, published *Woman's Wrongs*. She certified Jesus' enlightened opposition to home-making and contrasted it with the backwardness of Paul: "Paul could never quite get out of his mind the notion of woman's sphere. Into the mind of Christ it never came. Paul admonished women to guide the house. Jesus applauded a woman for not guiding the house." The coexistence of rival dogmas in the American atmosphere signified that by the last quarter of the nineteenth century radical domesticity was both firmly entrenched and imminently threatened.

The outcome of this competition in the marketplace of feminine philosophies was by no means the sole determinant of woman's fate. Political and economic realities counted for more, and the aftereffects of the Civil War were crucially felt everywhere. As Northern troops pulled out of the South, permitting a revitalized racism, a new army of women were occupying white collar jobs in the North and West, inspiring a revitalized sexism. Working women in mills and factories had for several decades suffered long hours, low wages, and many forms of exploitation; now their genteel counterparts at the typewriter and switchboard confronted a more insidious discrimination. They were often consigned to the backwater of spinsterhood and, if they went so far as to enter the professions, were accused of unfeminine behavior.

It seemed that every victory had its counterpart in some defeat. The era popularly thought to offer women the greatest degree of independence they had yet enjoyed—the 1920's—gave birth to the image of the carefree, hedonistic, thoroughly male-oriented female, the antithesis of today's liberated woman. Even when in later years career and marriage were occasionally thought to be compatible, those who sought both found that society's resistance took new form in the flagrant deficiency of child-care facilities and household assistance.

Yet all along there were women who declined to be discouraged by setbacks or stereotypes. They sought self-expression in their life together, as well as in their families. They welcomed new challenges eagerly while continuing to fulfill traditional roles. Their charm, stamina, and versatility are emblazoned across the pages that follow. Through the insights of the camera we come to understand afresh what it meant to be a woman in America.

I. Growing Up

2

The American girl has often seemed the most privileged of creatures. Adored by her parents, indulged by her brothers, worshipped by her suitors and revered by the world, she has traditionally—from Daisy Miller to Gatsby's Daisy—embodied freedom and grace, along with a certain appealing perversity.

But not all our young women were raised in a heady atmosphere of uncritical admiration. The daughters (as well as the sons) of blacks, immigrants, the poor, and the laboring classes relied for approval on their usefulness in the home and, upon adolescence, on their ability to increase the family income. Often enough, immigrant laborers arrived without their families; hence, as with the young Oriental pictured on one of the following pages, scarcity could, for a time, give children a special cachet. For the most part, however, Americans looked upon children as additional manpower on the farm or as potential wage earners. In some ways the role of girls was more arduous than that of boys, for they were often additionally charged with caring for younger siblings and managing the household, particularly in families where the mother had died prematurely, a common enough occurrence.

Beyond their economic value, the presence of children in the household was a source of joy, sometimes inspiring the parental indulgences reflected in the Christmas photograph. The loss of children, on the other hand, was a recurrent sorrow, and the photograph of the departed infant is a reminder that in the days before modern pediatric medicine the pregnant woman had almost as much to fear as to hope for. And successful delivery and survival of childhood illnesses were only the beginning of the journey for parents. Bringing children into responsibility required the firm patience and vigilance prescribed in the many Victorian forerunners of current child-rearing manuals.

The Calvinist concept of original sin had undergone significant revision by the middle of the nineteenth century. Children were no longer thought to have the stubbornly resistant natures

2.   A quick gulp.

3.   Tea for Two.

4

attributed to them by the Puritans, and the process of child-rearing —whether by an older sister or by the mother herself—was invested with tender pleasures unknown to the experts of earlier generations.

A more flexible outlook was initiated in 1842 with Horace Bushnell's *Christian Nurture* and was perpetuated in the 1890s by liberal thinkers like Mrs. Hannah Whitall Smith, author of *The Science of Motherhood*. Accommodation to the child's temperament overruled the harsh precepts of colonial days. This revolution in child psychology was to culminate in the twentieth century with the educational philosophy of John Dewey. It produced a less inhibited, more fearlessly individualistic young American, and it ultimately contributed to a relaxation of sexual stereotyping.

Training at home was increasingly complemented by training at school. Little girls sometimes began their education as early as age two in a "dame school" such as the one described in Lucy Larcom's *A New England Girlhood*. There they not only learned their letters but were indoctrinated into the differential treatment that they would thereafter experience. Miss Larcom recounted the unequal punishments meted out to the sexes: Boys were required to sit on an uncomfortable log instead of a bench, while girls were only given "an occasional rap on the head with the teacher's thimble." Early in their lives girls were taught that they were the weaker sex, intellectually as well as physically.

In time that assumption came to be questioned. Young women of the intellectual caliber of Margaret Fuller and Elizabeth Cady Stanton, under the influence of fathers who exposed them to ideas and learning, proved to themselves and to confirmed skeptics that they could function with ease in the worlds of scholarship and public affairs. Though they were both born too early to enjoy the benefits of a college education, succeeding generations, like those represented in the photographs of Smith and Barnard women, were luckier. Growing pains would always accompany the process of maturation in both sexes, but the confidence that made it possible to overcome them—or even to capitalize upon them— was now becoming more accessible to women.

4 and 5.   The infant of homesteading Montana parents might have been far better off in her coffee-box carriage than the children of the rich. According to Mrs. Julia McNair Wright, author of *The Complete Home,* an 1879 manual on household management, nursemaids often endangered the lives of their charges. "The nurse, chatting with her friends, or hastening to overtake a companion, dashes the little buggy over curbs and crossings. I have *even seen* a child flung bodily out of its carriage by such a jolt. In our parks I have seen maids rushing the little buggies down slopes, over drains, around curves, in a manner to endanger the spines and brains of infants."

5

6

6 and 7.   Could it be that the little lady feeding the chickens on the farm had a more wholesome life than her overdressed counterparts enjoying an overstuffed Christmas in the city?

8

9

8.   While individual Oriental laborers arrived by the thousands, restrictive laws made the immigration of an intact family a rarity. Thus the few children in the early Chinese communities were especially doted on, like this lavishly attired little girl in San Francisco.

9.   This photograph was entitled "Helping Mother Wash." But was this industrious black child helping mother or having fun pretending she was mother herself? In 1900 the former was likelier to be the reality.

10.   A canning demonstration of the Boys' and Girls' Clubs at a 1923 4-H Fair in Michigan. Industriousness not only led to a happy life, it was a virtue in itself. And the work ethic is still with us.

10

11.   The death of a young child was a common tragedy of nineteenth-century family life, and the post-mortem photo a treasured memento. "I knew she was but as a withering flower,/That's here to day, perhaps gone in an hour;/Like as a bubble, or the brittle glass,/Or like a shadow turning as it was./More fool then I to look on that was lent,/As if mine own, when thus impermanent." —Anne Bradstreet, In memory of my dear grand-child Anne Bradstreet. Who deceased June 20, 1699, being three years and seven months old.

11

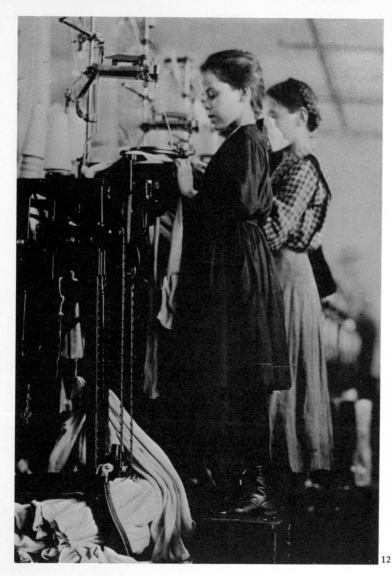

12

13

12.　From John Spargo's *The Bitter Cry of the Children* in 1906 to Robert Coles' *Children of Crisis* in 1964, Americans have felt a particular guilt about the victimization of children.

13.　"If I should die before I wake . . ."

14.　Consigned to a state welfare institution like this weeping pair, little girls seemed especially vulnerable.

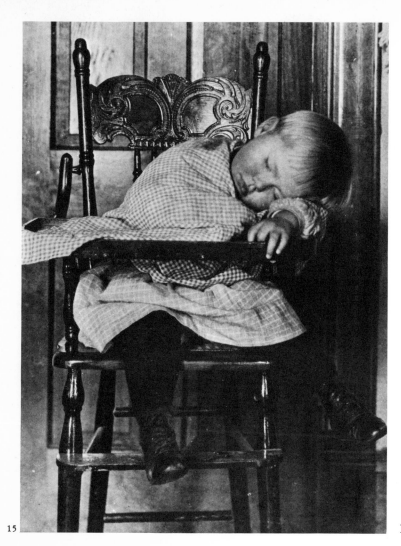

15

15.   Retreating into the private world of sleep.

16.   Window on a wintry world.

1 2 3 4 5 6 7 8
Mary Tufts.
Oscar
Alvin
Work while you work
And play while you
play.
That is the way to
be cheerful and gay

17.   Girls as well as boys benefited from the Jeffersonian ideal of a free public elementary education. This scene, identified as "The Last Day," depicts them celebrating the end of the school year and anticipating the joys of summer with equal glee.

18.   "No Labor, No Reward." Reaping the rewards of their labor at commencement in Black River Falls, Wisconsin in 1897.

19.   A studious class at an exclusive Boston finishing school.

20.   Sewing was an essential part of the curriculum.

20

21.   It took determination to tackle the scientific intricacies of a chemistry laboratory at Smith College.

21

22.   Sheathed in the dignity of their academic robes, these Barnard College students descend the grand staircase of Milbank Hall. Before 1910 more than a quarter of the women students in the country attended women's colleges.

22

II. Traditional Roles

23

23.   Women stayed close by their men's sides in a variety of improbable homes, sometimes in crude dugouts and remote cabins.

24.   Patient Griselda or the Wicked Wife of Bath? This bridegroom of 1925 will never know until the inner woman reveals herself in the course of married life.

In the photographs that illustrate women functioning in their traditional roles there is ample evidence (if it were needed) of the truism that woman's work is never done.

As they go about their familiar occupations at home and on the farm, the women on these pages seem to have substituted pride in immediate accomplishment for pride in long-term endeavor. Without women, they seem to ask, who would feed, clothe, and instruct the family? Who would clean the house and launder the clothes? These and other insistent features of household routine are almost lovingly celebrated. Yet we know that at moments of sudden confrontation with their potential selves, many women besides the indignant feminist Charlotte Perkins Gilman have denounced the wastefulness of household labor and have experienced the spiritual death that comes of contemplating dreary realities once too often.

In the nineteenth century and well into the twentieth, women had few alternatives. Not only was their universe constructed of everyday tasks that brought little permanent satisfaction, they were led to believe that home life was the grandest fate that could await them. In the early 1800's Eliza Southgate, a thoughtful young New Englander, wrote in a letter that, were she a man, she would "not be content with moderate abilities—nay, I should not be content with mediocrity in anything, but as a woman I am equal to the generality of my sex, and I do not feel that great desire of fame I think I should if I was a man." Decades later women were still expected to content themselves with modest aspirations and take their greatest pleasure in the opportunity to serve others.

A major paradox of woman's existence has been that she has come to love and honor the means of her own oppression. Housekeeping, elevated both to a spiritual calling and a quasi-exact science, became a chief source of women's self-respect and emotional gratification. Catharine Beecher, the leading nineteenth-century spokeswoman for this philosophy, sought throughout a lifetime to institutionalize her theories of domestic culture. In the

25

process she established schools and promoted a variety of educational schemes. She also grew to be an influential public figure a reveled in the power politics her work entailed. In the midst of busy life she commented: "I could do twice as much *head* work I could have the gentle exercise and the *amusement* of hous keeping. . . ." Ironically, this advocate of the all-encompassi seriousness of domestic labor privately looked upon it as a refres ing respite from her "real" work.

Few women could afford that luxury. For them it was neith exercise nor amusement. They handled not only housekeeping b the myriad duties of helpmeet, matriarch, and medical missiona to their families with strong nerves and determined optimis Whether feeding the farmhands in the nineteenth century banishing the ring around the suburban collar in the twentie they were assigned their tasks by men, not by themselves or ev by other women. And they learned to take joy in simple necessitie sewing together, searching for the best bargain, canning, weavin and raising baby chicks for sale to help the household econom They were ceaselessly inventive and passed their knowledge, li their recipes, on from mother to daughter. They were equal unpredictable family crises as well as to the predictable roles family teacher and corresponding secretary. They were love friends, advisers, and, above all, mothers.

Perhaps it is the knowledge that their labors are unendi that has given women a sense of being victims of time rather th masters of it, seldom able to create works that are universal a timeless. Could it be that women have for so long been in thrall time that only with great difficulty have they succeeded in escapi it, denying it, and ultimately, in the shape of a masterpiec defying it?

If so, it is understandable. Self-sacrifice, not creativity, w thought the appropriate heroic mode for women and, througho the nineteenth and early twentieth centuries, popular ideologi strengthened existing social prejudices. Slowly women saw that accepting such a view of themselves they were sacrificing anoth self, the self of talent, imagination, and intellect. The effort rescue that other self would become another route to heroism.

25.   No matter how poor the household, the wife was expected to be a good hostess. Here is a special guest—the local minister.

26.   An evening in the family circle, presided over by a watchful male.

26

27.   Sunday dinner was a weekly ritual.

28.

28.   Preparing the evening meal was a wife's daily task.

29.   On a summer day in the South, a pause in the day's occupations.

30.   Keeping children in close view as Mother tends to chores.

31.

31.   The history of women's labor is often the history of child care as well.

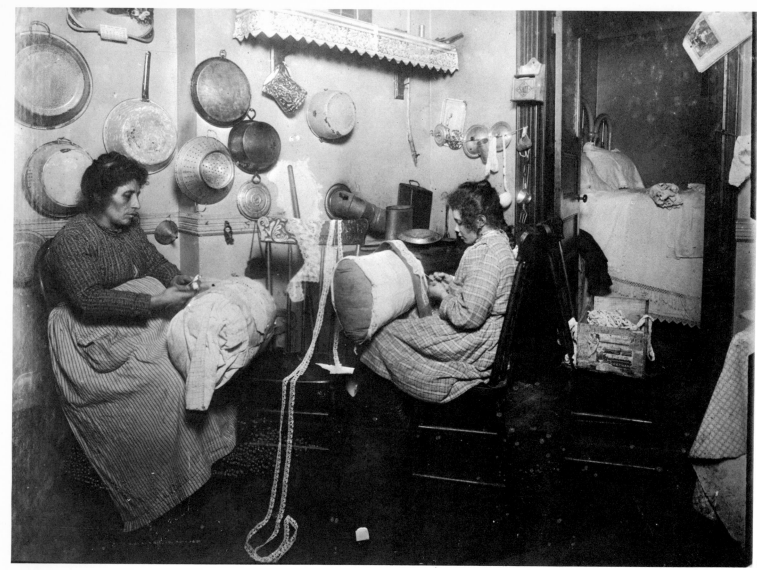

32. Mothers working with their daughters on handicrafts pass on skills and secrets.

33.   Mothers not only gave help but received it from their children.

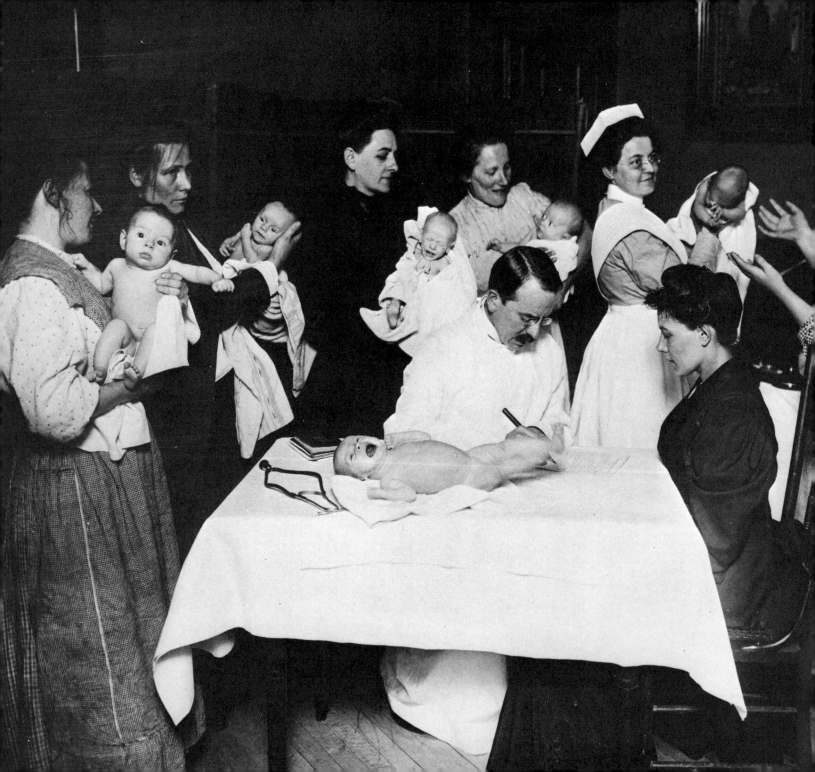

34. Caretakers of their children's health, mothers line up eagerly with their children at an early Infant Welfare Clinic in Chicago. As early as 1869 Catharine Beecher and Harriet Beecher Stowe warned against medical ignorance in their best-selling *The American Woman's Home:* "There is no point where a woman is more liable to suffer from a want of knowledge and experience than in reference to the health of a family committed to her care. Many a young lady . . . with little or no preparation has found herself the principal attendant in dangerous sickness, the chief nurse of a feeble infant, and the responsible guardian of the health of a whole family."

35. In Florida, a determined maternal search for "Florida Fleas."

35

37

36.   An early version of the nuclear family.

37.   In the days of the extended family, Grandmother was the best friend of all.

39

38.   Cleanliness may have been next to godliness, but it always required the dedication of woman.

39.   The exertions of doing the wash were sometimes assisted by hollowed-out tree trunks.

40.   The advent of the washboard did not reduce the need for women's labor.

40

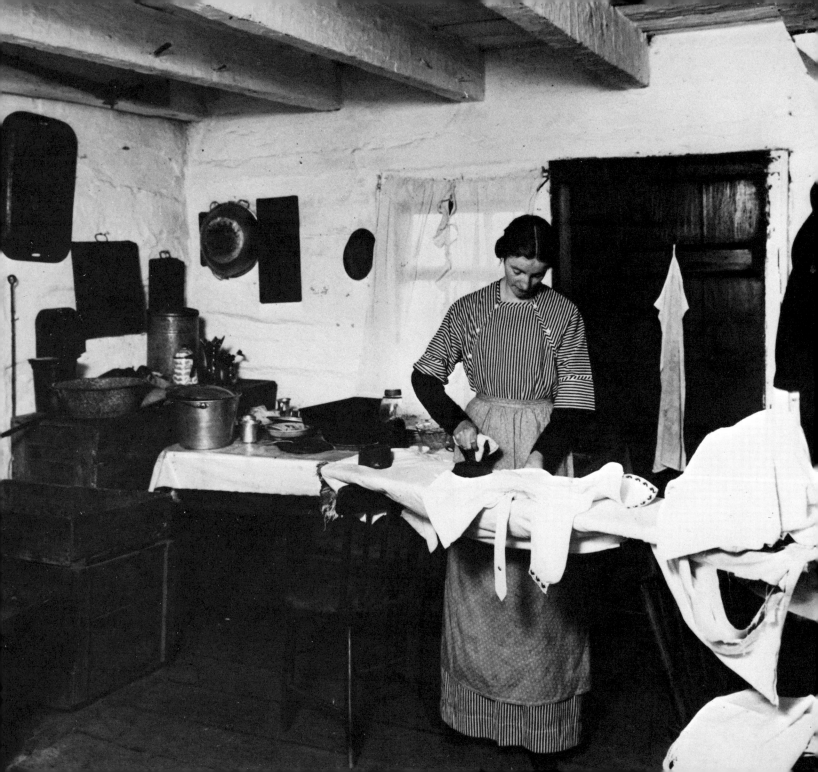

41.   This Virginia woman in a 1919 country kitchen appears resigned to her inescapable routine.

42 and 43.   "Progress in civilization has been accompanied by progress in cookery." —Fannie Merritt Farmer, *The Boston Cooking-School Cook Book,* 1896 (revised edition, 1918).

44, 45, and 46.　　"Cleaning is continuous."
—Charlotte Perkins Gilman, *The Home,* 1903.

47

48

49

47.   Churning in North Carolina.

48.   Slicing in Minnesota.

49.   At the time the Crow Indians on reservations received cattle as food rations from the federal government, it was the woman's job to clean the entrails.

50.   Women were a perpetual presence on the American agricultural landscape.

III. Working Women

51.   Carrying her take-home work, this woman was one of thousands of newly arrived immigrants who had little choice other than a work day of twelve to fourteen hours.

52.   Schoolteachers, like this one pictured helping her small charges master spelling in Idaho, were part of the growing female corps of underpaid and overworked moral agents in the classroom.

Legend has it that women are intended not to labor themselves but to be the beneficiaries of men's industry and solicitude. The legend dies hard. Working women, including working wives, have been a steady presence on the American scene but they have preferred to regard their labor as supplementary, temporary, and essentially expedient.

Indeed, women have even conspired with men to give their employment the trappings of gentility. In the 1830's and 1840's the cotton mills of Lowell, Massachusetts, employed young women from middle-class families at low wages and created a much-admired boarding-house culture with its own magazine, *The Lowell Offering.* In fact, the Lowell system promoted economic exploitation in the guise of literary self-improvement. While at first the mill workers themselves believed they were engaged in an uplifting experiment, later, at Lowell and elsewhere, women began to protest their working conditions, but they found few who would hear them.

Employers almost always thought of women as an easily replaceable labor force and therefore could afford to remain indifferent to their pleas. Leonara M. Barry, a labor organizer of the 1880's, described the condition of New York sewing-women in these words: "I can truthfully say that more injustice, scheming, trickery, and frauds of all kinds are practiced upon the helpless, poverty-bound sewing-women of New York City by the greedy, heartless employer than on any other class of wage-workers on the American continent." Such exposés had little effect, in part because of the habitual resistance of industry to labor reform, but also because women were reluctant to engage in sustained efforts to challenge a system that they persisted in believing was not central to their lives.

The reflections of this attitude are captured in the photographs of untroubled women engaged in everything from weighing metal coils to teaching children how to spell. For it did not matter whether women were in heavy industry or the nurturing

arts: Their resentment at being overworked and underpaid, when it did exist, seldom surfaced in forthright action.

Ultimately their consciousness was aroused, especially in the garment trades. There, abuses were most notorious: unregulated labor, exhausting piecework, injurious working conditions, overbearing employers. All these and more were stoically tolerated until strong leaders like Rose Schneiderman and organizations like the Women's Trade Union League became champions of working women.

More resistant to organizing efforts was the field of domestic service. Though it usually took a heavy economic and physical toll, especially on black women, it had the advantage of familiarity. Women used the skills and worked in the surroundings that coincided with their own experience, and this made it a popular employment stopgap for needy women. The Kansas boarding house scene suggests the positive spirit with which it was possible and sometimes necessary to perform such labor. Indeed, one might ask how our society would have functioned without the practiced hands of thousands of such willing women.

But domestic service was the one area of employment where women took their orders from other women and, as such, was least valued. The management of servants required decisiveness

53.　When more professional attention was not available, people depended on the watchful care of the home nurse.

and a certain emotional distance, two qualities that women, deprived of "worldly" experience, often lacked. Hence the "servant problem" which darkened the pages of housekeeping manuals of the nineteenth century. Upper class women often treated domestics shabbily because they felt threatened by their own dependence upon them; or, conversely, they envied the cook's or the maid's growing intimacy with husbands and children. Hence it was the rare domestic who enjoyed both respect and independence. Scarcity might have alleviated their situation, as illustrated during the 1849 gold rush, when one miner complained that his washwoman had "condescended" to do his washing "for $6 per dozen." But the regular arrival of immigrant women, especially those from Ireland, delayed any significant shift in the working conditions of domestics.

Though broader employment opportunities and equal pay still elude women, corrective legislation and an acceptance of women's capacity to perform almost any job as competently as men have greatly improved the lot of working women. Such progress, however, does not say it all. The photograph of the lunch break dance at the Royal Corset Factory in Worcester reminds us of the touchingly good-humored accommodation of working women to their conditions and of the lighthearted companionship that is almost always possible even in the midst of toil.

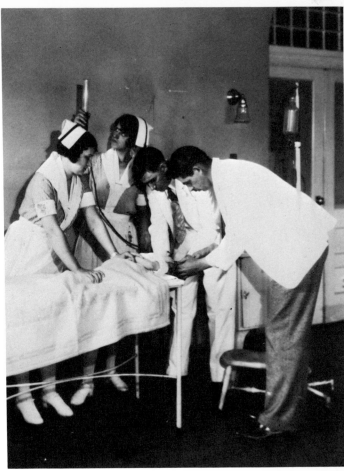

54. An intelligent and assertive young woman could become a trained nurse. A new profession for women had opened up.

54

55.   With the appearance of settlement houses in the late-nineteenth century, visiting nurses looked after the ailing city dweller, sometimes risking a climb over tenement roofs to reach their destination sooner.

56.   Serving meals in a Kansas boarding house, women could be paid for the skills they had learned in their homes.

58

57.   Now that they have picked the
cotton, these women are waiting to have
it weighed.

58.   Even the most unskilled could
always take in laundry, as in this wash camp
in the South.

59 and 60.   Indians, here the Northwest basket weaver and the Navajo rug weaver, used their age-old skills to combine domestic needs with irreplaceable artisanship.

62

61 and 62.   White collar workers of an
earlier era: women taking a Civil Service
typing exam in Chicago in 1909, and a full-
fledged typist in the City Treasurer's office
in Seattle in 1908. By 1890 the number of
girls graduating from high school was
double that of boys, making them natural
candidates for the clerical occupations
opening up in major cities across the country.

63

63.   Operating a switchboard, as these women in Richmond in 1884 are doing, was a job more and more sought after for its respectable status.

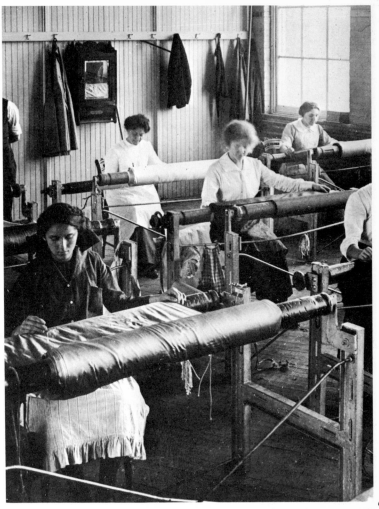

64.

64. Women with little formal education were trained on the job to operate a wide variety of machines.

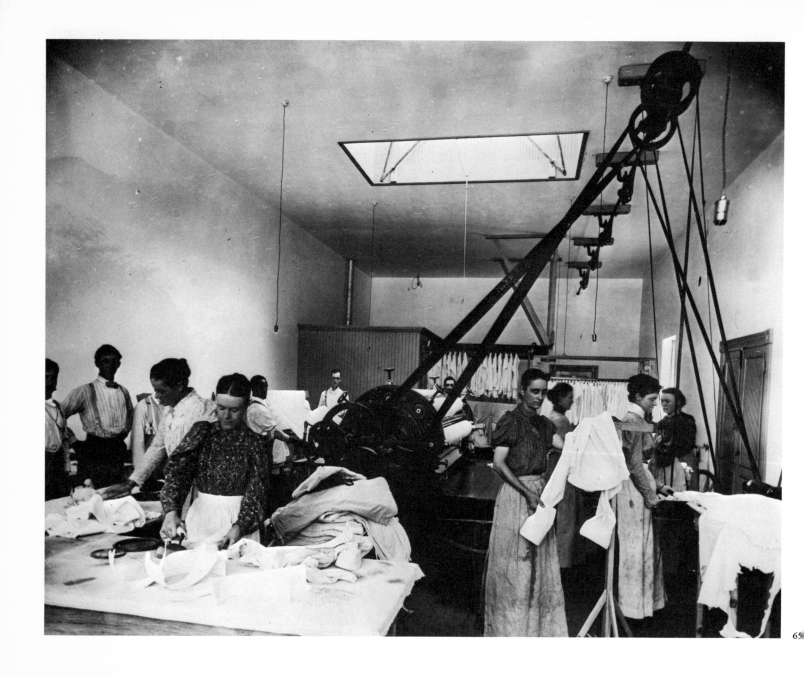

65

66

65.   Commercial laundries meant greater
efficiency, but they depended on the labor of
women who could withstand the sweltering
heat of their working environment.

66.   In their homes as well as in factories,
women were paid by the piece.

67 and 68.   World War I required an
unprecedented expansion of industry.
Women rose to the challenge, canning meat
and weighing metal coils. They adapted
their attire to the needs of the factory, as
these caps and culottes illustrate.

69.   In the textile mills of Massachusetts young women could be cultivated as well as hard-working. Here we see them leaving the mill at the end of the day with a male escort at hand.

70.   The strict self-discipline of the daily barre could be as demanding as any kind of men's work.

71.   The Royal Corset Company in
Worcester, Massachusetts, either encouraged
or permitted its female employees to frolic
about like this during their lunch break.

IV. Diversions

72.   Whether she is worried about some new wrinkles or simply pleased with what she sees, this woman is absorbed in an ancient pastime—self-scrutiny.

73.   A collective hair wash, or drying off after a swim? Swimming for fun and refreshment became popular for women only in relatively modern times. Having taken the plunge, that is, gotten into the swim, the ladies proceeded to let their hair down.

Sports, games, and simple forms of relaxation provided happy moments of relief from routine duties and, possibly, a fresh outlook on life. The photographs that follow suggest some of these forms of rejuvenation.

74.   Oh that splendid adventure—a ride
in the car! But the wind and the dust—
better be prepared!

75.   Photographs of Indian squaws usually portray them as serious people. Here they are playing serious poker.

75

76.   Angling for trout, or whatever, was
a demanding sport. These outfits were not
likely to make it easier.

77.   Like tennis, golf would require all the power a lady could come up with. Would that make her less a lady?

78.   Practiced in keeping their balance in other ways, women tried for poise on their bicycles as well.

78

79.   Shooting an arrow into the air had become, by the 1920's, a matter, not of romance, but of fairly fierce competition.

79

V. Togetherness

80

Sisterhood is a modern slogan for a centuries-old habit. Togetherness among women took many forms in America—teas and quilting bees and lawn parties, of course. But the moods reflected in the photographs that follow may not always have been so tame. Witness croquet: How many of those wooden balls had a husband's, or a father's, or a "suitable" suitor's face on them as the studious ladies wound up for a solid resounding whack? It may have been after such exhausting forays that they permitted themselves an hour of repose, napping on a carefully tended lawn, their fans aside, wicker rockers supporting them, and an ample urn benignly gazing from above.

Toasting the bride-to-be in champagne or coping with the suffering of the social outcast, they were spreading a newly wrought image of solidarity across the continent that they had recently helped open up, and they were taking strength in doing it together. Whether their mood was grave or frivolous, it had an unmistakable air of sisterly affinity.

In the nineteenth century women were increasingly relegated to their separate sphere, but the full consequences of this isolation were not foreseen by the men who perpetrated it. Sewing circles, for example, could become the breeding ground for feminist ideas, yet they continued to symbolize respectability because needlework itself had the incontestable stamp of virtue. Sarah Josepha Hale, editor of the influential *Godey's Lady's Book,* advised that "there is nothing degrading or dishonoring to the highest social position in a thorough and complete knowledge of plain sewing. No woman should grow up in ignorance of this most important art." Brought together at times by an excess of leisure and at other times by the pressures of economic necessity, as evidenced in the photographs that follow, women welcomed what characterized their life together: a sense of relief from the male universe.

80.   "Do not rejoice in conquests, either that your power to allure may be seen by other women, or for the pleasure of rousing passionate feelings that gratify your love of excitement." —Margaret Fuller, *Woman in the 19th Century,* 1845. These sentiments are gleefully ignored at a triumphant Bridesmaids' Dinner in 1905.

81.   Did togetherness not only help women face the hard realities of their lives but also promote dreams and illusions?

82.   The rigors of an ocean voyage, such
as this one on the S.S. *Penland* in 1893, are
made tolerable by the mutual support
offered by fellow immigrants.

Often, too, they experienced the special mental exhilaration generated by the absence of familiar authority. The "consciousness-raising" of the contemporary women's movement is in fact the culmination of a long history of intellectual togetherness, beginning in the seventeenth century with Anne Hutchinson's religious assemblies, where women were encouraged to question male interpretations of the Bible. Two centuries later Margaret Fuller, who was thought by a number of her male contemporaries to possess one of the finest intellects of their time, held a series of transcendental "conversations" with the wives of prominent Bostonians and eager bluestockings thirsting for enlightenment. Metaphysical, artistic, historical, and educational themes were explored together and a state of exaltation often ensued.

Fuller's thoughts on the relations between the sexes encouraged women to disregard male assumptions about them and to value their individual natures. Male tyranny was not, however, the sole obstacle to self-realization in her eyes. She recognized the petty ways in which women frequently did themselves in. In an essay on "Household Nobleness" she warned against gossiping females being cruelly critical of each other's housekeeping and risking their friendships for "spots on the table-cloth" that "were more regarded than those they made on their own loyalty and honor in the most intimate relations."

In many ways women's relations with each other were indeed the most intimate they enjoyed. In a world that gave men continual psychological support and countless confirmations of their own value, women could often gain precious confidence only from one another. In work, at rest, at home, and in society, togetherness became the means by which they were released from the weariness of uninspiring tasks and energized for more challenging ones.

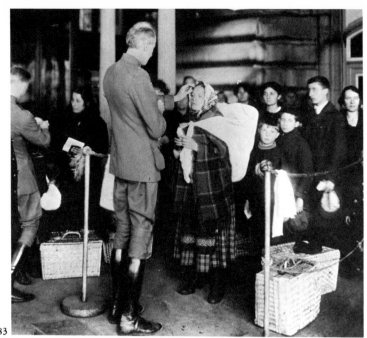

83

83. The entry point examination at
Ellis Island determines one's fate: into the
new world or back to the old?

84

84. The Italian bread peddlers on Mul-
berry Street are a reassuring sight to recent
women arrivals.

85.   With minimal integration into the American society around them, the Chinese women of San Francisco maintained their own ways and gave the city some of its exotic atmosphere.

86 and 87.   Women sewing: One of these professional dressmakers has contrived to install herself in genteel surroundings, while the other two manage in a tenement.

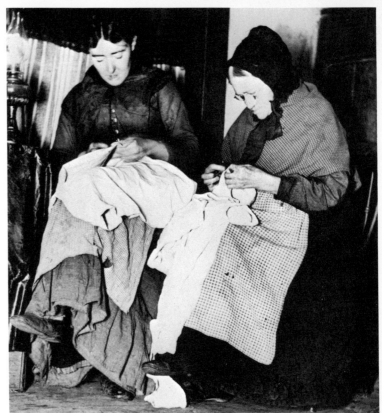

88

88.　"The Writer is of opinion, that tea and coffee are a most extensive cause of much of the nervous debility and suffering endured by American women . . ." —Catharine Beecher, *A Treatise on Domestic Economy,* 1841. Many years after Beecher's warning, tea was still a time of togetherness.

89.　Far from suffering from nervous debility, the women in this Turkish Bath Club in New York in 1904 seem to be expiring of sheer physical contentment.

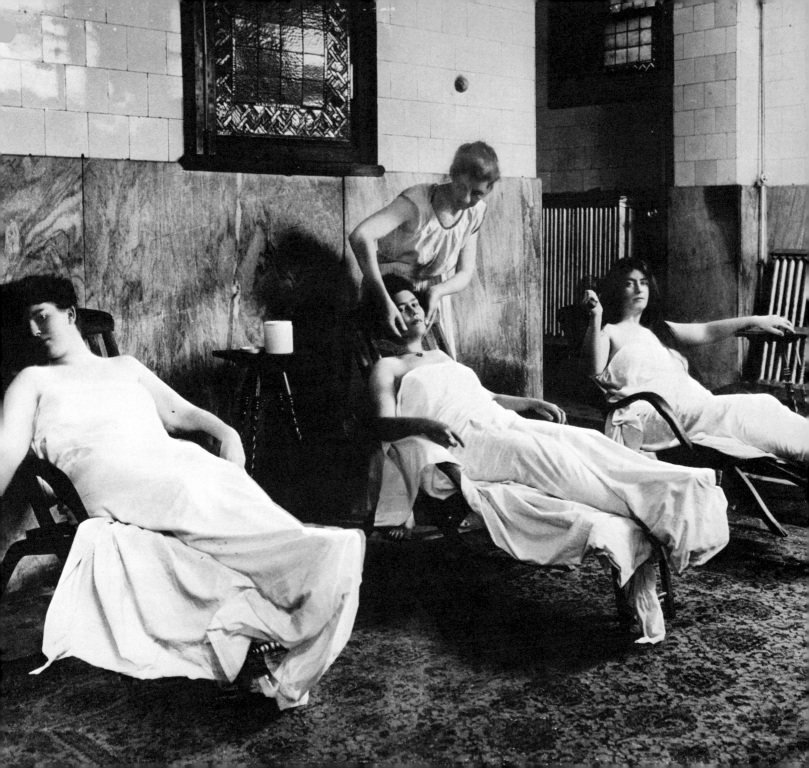

90

91

90.   Sharing the shock of sudden disaster during the San Francisco earthquake.

91.   Huddled together in mutual misery, these women temporarily occupying a "police station lodge" are caught by social reformer Jacob Riis's compassionate camera.

92.   With untimely death still a commonplace experience in their lives, women shared their grief.

93

93.   In the 1850's a cultivated young
black woman named Charlotte Forten
interrupted the troubled thoughts in her
diary to comment: "Rode to the sewing
circle at the Jameses. The largest and
pleasantest we've ever had. Enjoyed myself
very much." Half a century later, another
sewing sisterhood.

94.   What could be more satisfying than
a good meal in the company of old friends?

94

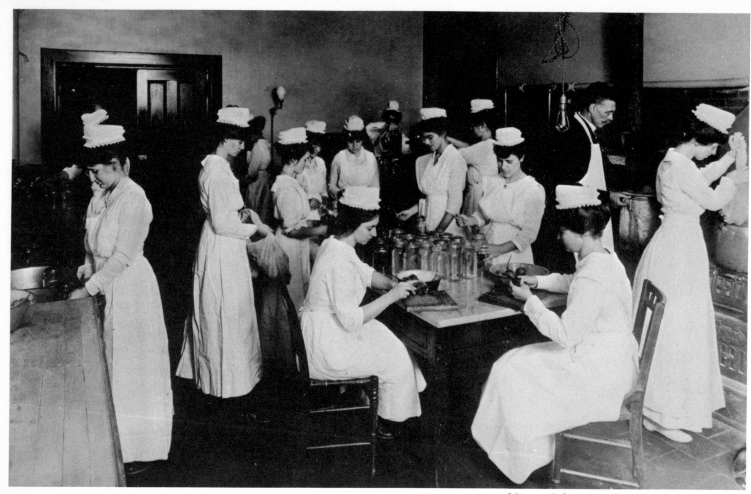

95.   A footnote in Lucy Maynard Salmon's *Domestic Service,* first published in 1897, might have inspired these students in a canning class: "Mrs. L, living on a farm in a Southern city, has built up 'an exceedingly remunerative business' by selling to city grocers preserves, pickles, cakes, and pies."

96.   Searching for the best bargain was a
duty, a challenge, and an escape from the
confines of home.

97. This scene of a lawn party in Columbus, Nebraska in 1905 echoes the idyllic American landscape recorded in Louisa May Alcott's *Little Women*: "A pleasant green field, with three wide-spreading oaks in the middle and a smooth strip of turf for croquet."

VI. Women With Men

98

In the very "otherness" of the opposite sex and the enigma of the sexual bond, women have discovered some of the features of their own identity. As these photographs witness, they have worked, played, rested, grown, and ventured new worlds with the men in their lives. They have known each other's strengths and failings; they have been each other's nemesis and blessing. In the open and fluid society of America opportunities for emotional growth and a rewarding mutuality have been more available than anywhere else, yet myths and stereotypes have multiplied, and the sexual landscape has been disfigured with misconceptions, hostilities, and, at times, outright warfare.

Through this perpetual haze certain couples have loomed as legends. In our own day they have included Scott and Zelda Fitzgerald, Eleanor and Franklin Roosevelt, Anne and Charles Lindbergh, John and Jacqueline Kennedy. They became legendary not because their lives were always harmonious, nor even so much because they were individually remarkable, but because each offered precisely the qualities which complemented those of the other. And despite increasing fragmentation of the family, a burgeoning divorce rate, and styles of living that challenge the inevitability of monogamous and exclusive heterosexuality, marriage remains the preferred arrangement among men and women.

In the nineteenth century it hardly resembled our contemporary ideal. Alexis DeTocqueville, perhaps the greatest student of our society, observed that marriage invariably tamed the independence of the American girl and reduced her horizons to home and family. This abrupt domestication required her acquiescence in socially assigned roles and discouraged the mutual exploration of personality that today's couples seek both inside and outside marriage.

But the couple was only one of the many forms which contained women's relationship to men, and it should not obscure the others. Seated at the soda fountain, travelling in the parlor car, or

98.   Side by side in the midst of the bustling commercial life of Hester Street on the Lower East Side of New York.

99.   With the wearisome ocean voyage over, these women on Ellis Island face their American futures with their menfolk.

making merry at a formal party, each sex encountered the other in distinct groups and circumstances. Numbers were a protection against the pressures of choice and the risks of self-revelation. They made possible the easiest retreats—and the safest overtures.

Perhaps no friendship with male contemporaries could quite substitute for the special closeness of a cherished brother. But the most crucial of her relationships with men may have been a woman's with her father. Jane Addams, founder of the settlement house and lifelong champion of the underprivileged, attributed a shaping influence to her father's abhorrence of inequality and his rigorous honesty with himself. Similar testimonials are scattered across the pages of many a distinguished female's autobiography. Yet fathers could be a source of irritation as well as inspiration. In "Woman's True Duty," an admonitory tale which appeared in *Miss Leslie's Magazine,* the dutiful heroine asks of her moral counselor what she might do to please her father, and is told: "Your father is fond of music; a song from you would delight him when he returns wearied from his counting-house. Yet I have heard you refuse to sing for him." The daughter's reply is couched in the polite accents of her time but expresses a thoroughly contemporary impatience: "That was wrong I confess—but he always asks for old songs, such as were the fashion thirty years ago; if he would listen to my new music— —"

Whether husbands, brothers, friends, or fathers, men have suffused women's lives as much in little ways as in the consequential ones. Occasionally they disappointed and perplexed, sometimes they surprised and delighted. Frequently they were a problem and, just as frequently, a solution.

100. Black women in South Carolina join their men in the trek home after a day in the cotton fields. Unable to protest their lot, they were dependent, before the Civil War, on the consciences of other women. Angelina Grimké, a wealthy white native of South Carolina, became their leading spokeswoman. She urged other women to "try to persuade your husband, father, brothers, and sons that slavery is a crime *against God and man.*"

100

101.   The artist is apparently trying to gain total grasp of his inspiration. The model seems to be controlling her responses successfully.

102.   What can possibly have led to this particular confrontation of the sexes? And what transpired afterward?

103 and 104.   Playing cards from a hammock in Ohio and bathing off Long Island—each offered the pleasure of one-to-one companionship.

104

105.   Fifty years after this photograph
was shot in an innocent drugstore soda
fountain, this scene would take place in a
singles bar.

106. Gazing in unison from the pier.
The collective encounter was a frequent
preliminary to closer acquaintanceships.

107.   Ice-skating—a perfect opportunity
for gentlemen to demonstrate their skill and
daring and solicitousness and for ladies to
show how helpless they were.

108.   Do these two women prefer, like Gertrude Stein, to sit with their backs to the view, and have they run out of conversation while waiting for lunch to be caught?

109.   "It is easy, indeed, to perceive that
even amid the independence of early youth
an American woman is always mistress of
herself; she indulges in all permitted
pleasures without yielding herself up to
any of them, and her reason never allows
the reins of self-guidance to drop, though
it often seems to hold them loosely."
—Alexis de Tocqueville, *Democracy in
America,* 1840.

110.   Bouncing along in a parlor car on the Northwestern Railroad must have been a splendid way to get acquainted. There were scenery and luxurious appointments, and the gentleman couldn't wander very far away.

111.   Entertaining eligible males at a chafing dish party.

11

112.   The formality of the attire seems not to have interfered with the informality of the mood at this party.

113.   Making beautiful music together.

114.   The contentment of companionship in the golden years.

VII. Women Alone

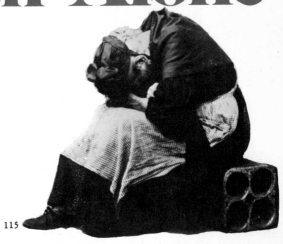

115.   The desolation of poverty in old age.

116.   Homesteader's Cabin, 1880's. "It is this very dearth of so many things that once made her life easy and comfortable which throws her back upon her own resources." —William W. Fowler, *Woman on the American Frontier,* 1879.

Solitude has traditionally accompanied a variety of feminine fates and has variously been a comfort, a threat, and a mark of honor. And while the spurned spinsters and helpless widows of the nineteenth century have been succeeded by the swinging singles and the dauntless divorcées of the twentieth, the burdens of child-care and earning a livelihood are still familiar problems for the woman alone. How often, whether in the past or today, has the divorced or widowed male parent—in contrast to the female parent—assumed sole responsibility for raising children, or launched a totally new career for himself in mid-life?

The marginality and emptiness of the solitary woman's life has been proverbial, but it is more accurately a historic prejudice. The homesteader and the women at the armory in the photographs in this section confronted a loneliness mixed with dread, but they learned to cope. The self-defense expert and the tightrope walker faced solitary danger, but they proved it could be taken in stride. Our past is in fact replete with examples of women who successfully went it alone.

Three who achieved permanent distinction as loners in their different ways were Susan B. Anthony, Margaret Sanger, and Gertrude Stein. Anthony lived the private life of the spinster but also the public life of continuous involvement in a cause—the drive for women's rights, in which she had the emotional support of scores of friends and associates. Margaret Sanger's private life did not lack for masculine attention, but her dedication to the then scandalous birth control movement often isolated her from the sympathy and support of the public. Gertrude Stein, surrounded by artist friends and her own lifelong companion, Alice B. Toklas, nonetheless sought the isolation of experimentalism in her writing. Far from being a detriment to them, the very ways in which these women experienced aloneness made possible their distinctive

legacies. Surely, for example, Anthony's singleminded concentration on her work at the expense of a family life made her the most effective figure in the women's rights movement.

It is of course true that when family ties were firmer than they are today, women expected to receive and give all kinds of help to those related to them by blood or marriage. The community, as well, in social, religious, or ethnic organizations, could usually be called upon in times of stress. Even in sparsely populated areas women instinctively responded to each other's needs, knowing that hardship or disaster rarely played favorites for long. These "support systems" are only now being defined and analyzed; formerly, they were the female's amorphous, and sometimes invisible, way of surviving.

Nonetheless, aloneness always remained in every woman's experience, from the adolescent suffering shyness to the elderly woman whose friends had died before her. The isolation, and the

117

117.   With her bonnet as protection from the harsh sun, this Southern frontierswoman cultivates her vegetable garden.

silence, that pervaded much of the daily routine of the frontier wife or the small-town "maiden lady" challenges the imagination of women accustomed to telephones, radios, television, and automobiles. In her moving journal, Alice James, the invalid sister of the novelist Henry and the philosopher William, recollected a year she had spent living alone. Her words express with bitter precision the anguish of many a woman consigned to separation from society: "How I longed to . . . escape from the 'Alone, Alone!' that echoed through the house, rustled down the stairs, whispered from the walls, and confronted me like a material presence as I sat waiting, counting the moments as they turned themselves from today to tomorrow."

While going it alone was not to be eradicated, the social and technological revolutions of this century have altered women's circumstances to such a degree that aloneness is now more often a choice than a distasteful destiny.

118.

118. The bespectacled entrepreneur tends her baby chicks. Selling them brought in some hard cash, but it was a risky business: Primitive methods of keeping them warm sometimes resulted in the house burning down.

119

119.　This elderly North Carolina woman addresses herself to the complexities of a massive hand loom.

120.

120.   An air of absorption envelops the artist who confirms Mrs. Priscilla Baird in her address on "Aesthetic Culture" delivered at the 1893 Congress of Women: "Can there be, is there any true culture where the aesthetic is ignored, or even neglected?"

121.   "French Jenny," a prostitute of 1895, had the weary air of one who had no illusions about either the pitfalls or the opportunities of her profession.

21

122.   The woman alone could learn to
cope with physical aggression. A well-aimed
umbrella worked wonders.

123.

123.   And so did a swiftly executed karate kick.

124.　　Set against the manufactured landscape, this boldly clad actress stares out into the void.

125.   Several women tightrope walkers braved Niagara and one even went over the falls in a barrel. Here Maria Spelterini defies the whirlpool rapids.

Lassie mending Soldiers Clothes
Front Line with Gen. Pershings Troops

126.   A Cheyenne woman, unassisted, puts up a lodge. Tribal tradition assigned this task to women.

127.   Following the Good Lady Festival in San Francisco this woman observes the ritual of burning sacramental banners. Only on rare religious holidays could Chinese women venture outside the home alone.

128.   Salvation Army women who performed domestic services for General Pershing's troops could anticipate loneliness as well as physical danger.

129.   Does this winsome young woman in a corset ad of 1903 project enough of her own charm to convince her public of the product's special merits? Some members of the older generation remained unconvinced: "What's the matter with women nowadays? . . . Having their pictures taken with nothing on but with what would be a clout around their middle or something that shows their shape! Makes me wish I could be a cow instead of a woman!"—Harriet Connor Brown, *Grandmother Brown's Hundred Years, 1827–1927.*

130.   A few moments of solitary reflection while dressing.

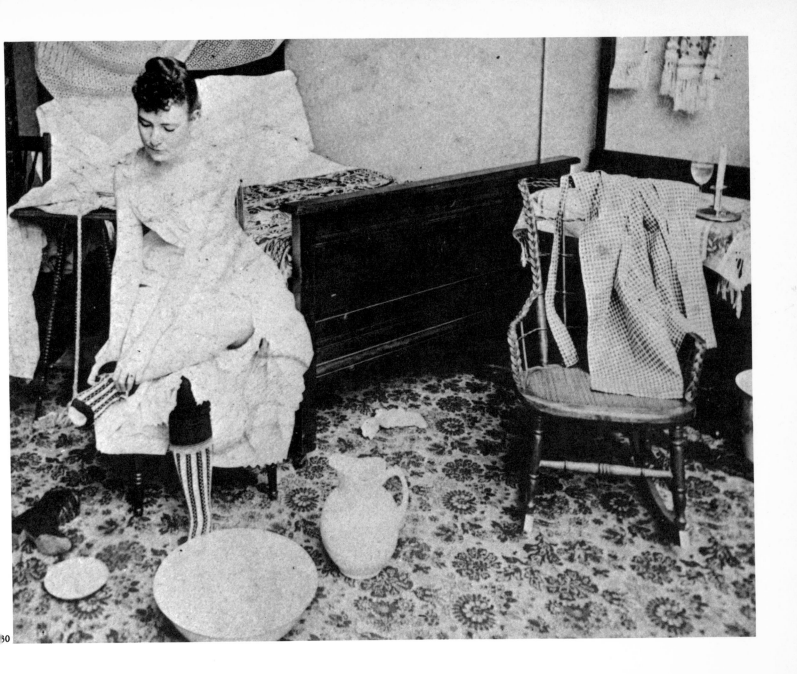

131.	Mrs. Leoni's New York parlor in the 1890's was an expression of her unique vision of beauty.

132.   At the armory the overwhelmingly male presence of this group of Spanish-American War soldiers leaves these women feeling their separateness as a sex.

133.   In the twilight years of an
unrevealed life history, a woman welcomes
tranquility and seems content with the
silences of solitude.

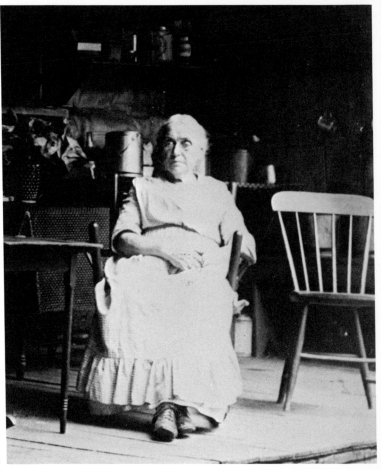

133

VIII. Stereotypes

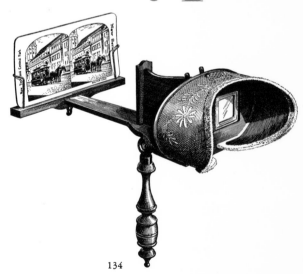

134

134 and 135.　　In the latter half of the nine-teenth and the early years of the twentieth centuries, a viewing device called the stereopticon and the stack of double pictures called stereoviews beside it were standard equipment in thousands of parlors. The illusion of three-dimensional realism in the "stereopticon views" provided the family with both amusement and instruction.

Here is a sampling from stereopticon views of a few of the ways in which women were standardized in the popular mind. These stereotypes deserve comparison with the realities of women's lives suggested by less contrived photographs.

136.   In 1903 stereoscopic sets like "Courtship and Marriage" were very popular. The first view of the series is of the smitten suitor.

136

137.   The second view shows the bride-to-be eavesdropping while her suitor asks her father for her hand in marriage.

7

138.   Next, a burlesque of the bachelor dinner.

138

139.   We observe the nervous bride about to be kissed.

139

140.   This final view exposes love's idyll, just deflated by the accusing maid.

141.   Another stereopticon view entitled "Women's Rights: The Rehearsal." An early version of role-reversal.

141

142.   And another: "Country Post-Office." Steaming open letters for the local gossip.

142

IX. Breakthroughs

143

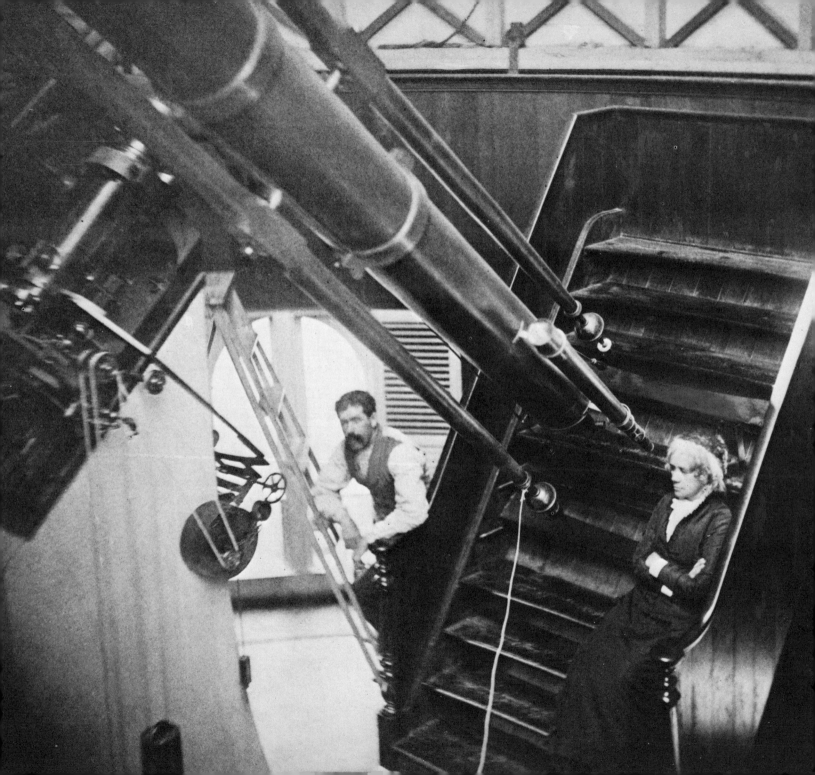

143.   The new chariots gave women an exhilarating sense of escape and power.

144.   Maria Mitchell discovered a new comet in 1847 and until 1943 was the only female elected to the American Academy of Arts and Sciences. She was for many years a much revered Professor of Astronomy at Vassar College and director of the observatory there.

The first American female breakthrough occurred in 1587, when Virginia Dare was born on Roanoke Island off the North Carolina coast, becoming the first native American daughter of immigrant English parents. While she, and all that little colony, dropped precipitously out of recorded history, her spiritual descendants have shattered other frontiers with better success. Scientists and farm hands, skillful repairers of cars and of teeth, jurors and pristine voters, seasoned guzzlers and gold-seekers, most of these women indicate by their postures or their gestures that they are not about to be written off as the weaker sex. Something new was happening to them, and it was sure to happen to their men-folk as well.

In our fixation on the attainment of suffrage as the culmination of a long struggle for recognition of women's rights, we forget that women were busy for decades asserting those rights before society caught up with them. And in our absorption with the protesters—from Carry Nation versus the saloonkeepers to Emma Goldman versus the business tycoons to Betty Friedan versus the male establishment—we are apt to neglect the more obscure doers, the women who took on the tough, risky, and unanticipated contests of life. They seldom kept diaries or wrote autobiographies, for their lives hardly permitted the luxury of reflection, but for brief moments their vigor and daring were captured by the eye of the camera.

The presence of the frontier was a continual reminder of how much in life could not be predicted or contained. American women rose to the demands of a world that was often catastrophic: Whether fighting off Indian raids or hiding runaway slaves, physical danger was a steady element of their moral landscape. The Scottish journalist Alexander Mackay commented that the whole course of the American girl's education "is one habitual lesson of self-reliance." Even in times of relative well-being, women were required to invent new solutions to problems presented by the unfamiliar prairie, forest, or desert. Medical expertise was seldom available, and the dangers of childbirth ever-present. The frequency of tragedy is memorialized in "gift books" expressly designed for women. In *The Rainbow* of 1847, the poet, Frances H. W. Green, confronted the death of a "Still-born Babe" with a defiant cry: "O, then, I am *not* childless. Thou art gone where angel-nurses bear thee."

The same spirit infused women who later fought for feminism, peace, and the right of self-expression. Reconciliation to reality did not appeal to them. Rather than accept the status quo, they openly attacked it; rather than mourn the absence of opportunities for their sex, they created new ones. Denial of insurmountable obstacles became, in fact, an essential emotional preliminary to constructive action.

The movement for women's rights, growing out of the exclusion of Elizabeth Cady Stanton and Lucretia Mott from participation in the World Anti-Slavery Convention in 1840, inspired a series of political breakthroughs for women. From small beginnings at organization they rallied large groups of women to the cause of suffrage, and a succession of forceful figures like Susan B. Anthony and Lucy Stone and later Carrie Chapman Catt and Alice Paul each played crucial parts in fostering the Nineteenth Amendment.

During the decades when suffrage was laboriously being fought for, women forced open the doors to many historically male professions. In addition they created settlement houses, formed labor unions, and operated businesses. While carrying on these activities, they seemed instinctively to avoid jeopardizing the special quality of their relationships with men. Foreign observers had repeatedly noted the easy cameraderie of relations between the sexes in America. In 1888, Lord Bryce astutely identified the other beneficiaries of the accelerating push toward sexual equality: "Men gain in being brought to treat women as equals rather than as graceful playthings or useful drudges." At the time of Bryce's comment traditional roles had certainly not been jettisoned, but the number and impact of feminine breakthroughs were already such that a new era seemed to be beckoning.

145.   In 1897 the irrepressible Martha Cannary Burk, better known as Calamity Jane, shares a companionable moment with these men outside a Montana bar. As late as 1913 the sociologist Elsie Clews Parsons observed: "In the United States the public water fountains are not differentiated for men and women, but 'bars' are invariably closed to women. Many clergymen preach an annual sermon against 'growing intemperance among women' and a drunken woman is universally held to be 'more disgusting' than a drunken man."

146.   "In many cases, where the 'weaker' sex are brought in direct rivalry of endurance with their sterner companions, they prove that they are at least equal; and when the difference of habit and occupation are taken into consideration, we are compelled to award the fresher laurels to woman."
—John Frost, *Pioneer Mothers of the West,* 1869.

146

147

147.   This hardy pair of prospectors on their way to the Klondike in the 1890's were among the intrepid adventurers to the Yukon and later to Nome City. Other women risked the journey to run hotels, open schools, and serve as nurses.

148

148.   Two denizens of what was euphemistically called a "Fancy House" in Dawson, another Gold Rush boom town.

149.   "Swearing in a Vote." From the
tiniest hamlet to the burgeoning cities,
women voted, but rarely as a bloc. While
failing to exert the powerful new influence
on national life that many hoped they
would, their presence nonetheless brought a
reformist impulse to state and local politics.

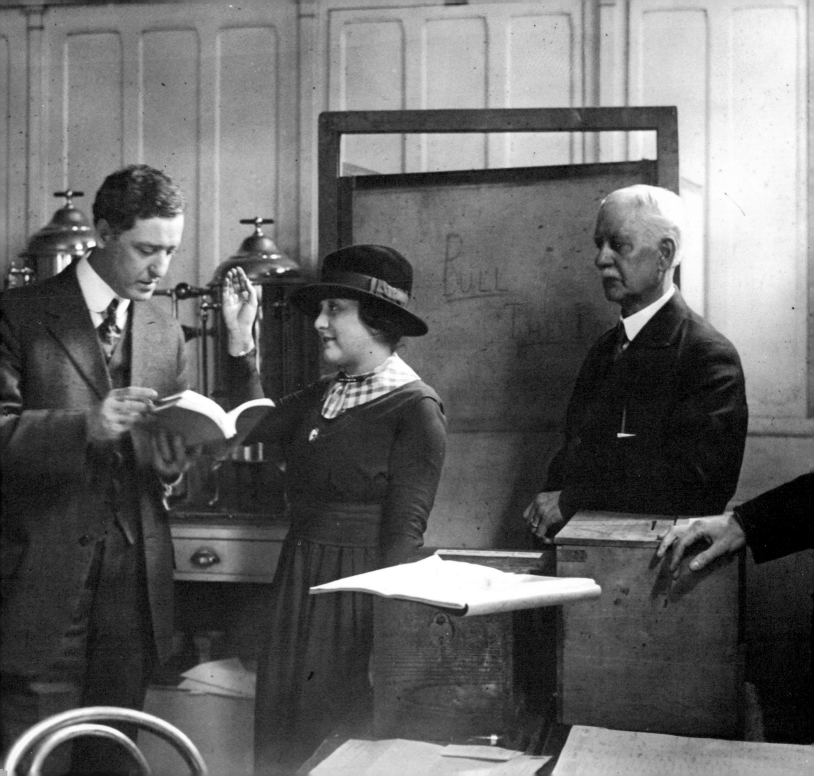

150.

150.   An early entrant into an exclusively male world, Dr. Olga A. Lentz, a dentist of 1910, illustrates the words of a successful female dental surgeon of the 1890's. When asked if she thought women could qualify as dental professionals, she replied: "In my opinion they are better fitted than men to make good dentists. The latter use too much force, and often crush a tooth or injure the jaw, in taking one out."

151.

151.   During the Shirtwaist Strike of 1910 women give each other psychological support at the New York headquarters of the Women's Trade Union League.

152. A dozen years before this first women's jury convened in 1910, Utah was the pioneer state in granting women the right to be jurors. But it was only as recently as 1966 that a federal district court ruled against Alabama's refusal to allow women to serve.

152

153. At a hotel bar in 1917 women demolish an old taboo.

153

154

154.   A guardian of morality checks the length of a bathing suit. In the 1920's skirts rose and corsets all but disappeared— a new freedom of the body to match the new freedoms of the mind.

155.   What the cowboys thought about this female riding in their rodeo is not recorded. Her own reaction is obviously one of intense elation.

156

156.   These farmerettes in World War I
testify that in times of emergency women
were well equipped to hold their own down
on the farm.

157

157.   Women entered the machine shop
with zest as industrial workers in World
War I, experiencing their first significant
shift from textile industries to metal trades.
Despite promises of being kept on, few
were offered the opportunity to apply their
skills once the war was over.

158.

158. Few jobs, not even that of auto mechanic, were so thoroughly the monopoly of men that they did not have women aspiring and able to fill them.

159.

159. The climate after World War I was favorable to the acceptance of women in the office. Rapid business growth increased the need for clerical workers, more young women were receiving high school educations, and the wartime example of married professional women made work outside the home seem respectable to a great many others.

160

160. Mrs. Sophie Parkinson employs a sure hand in demonstrating her blacksmithing skills in 1924.

161. Collie Colliers, a Chicago reporter, scales the dizzy heights in 1920.

X.Changing Images

162. These ladies have dared to venture on a perilous trip in a rowboat. Their parasols, hats, clothing—and much else—were already on their way downstream.

163. In an evocative pictorial image, maypoles and maidens in white dresses intermingle in the rites of an American spring.

The period from 1850 to 1930, especially the post-World War I years, saw startling changes in the public images of women. The photographs in the pages that follow suggest the evolution of some of these changes and illuminate the history that produced them. Rapid industrial advance, the growing importance of the consumer and of the service sector of the economy, the communications revolution, all these are among the familiar developments which had their effects upon the lives of women. Subtly, and not without controversy, the nineteenth-century view of woman was replaced by one which saw her more as a free agent and less as an exclusively domestic and maternal presence. Soon, radical feminists were not alone in viewing women as the potential saviors of humankind. From James Hegyessy's *Race Regeneration Through Woman* to Ashley Montagu's *The Natural Superiority of Women*, there were even men who believed that women's contribution was crucial, and that its fullest expression was not inconsistent with their equality.

The dialectical implications of this position were to be debated endlessly from the late 1960's on into the 1970's, when the movement for "women's liberation" flowered into the single most significant period of female consciousness in our history. But at the time these photographs were taken, women had little rehearsal for such an intense drama. They merely knew that, while images change, functions and fallacies often do not. Along with their freer life style they retained many of their old functions. Along with occasional concessions to their equality or even superiority, fallacies about their innate nature persisted. Most Americans were not ready to live with the idea that women were both different and equal.

In fact, a basic contradiction marked the way American women were regarded during the period of the photographs included in this volume. On the one hand, middle and upper class women were seen as fragile creatures, vulnerable to all sorts of physical and psychological infirmities, and steadily in need of protection, if not pampering. Working women, on the other hand, were expected to put in a lengthy day of exhausting toil without whimpering, or questioning why their pay, if any, was less than a man's.

Modern psychology has permanently shaken the notion that women are constitutionally more "emotional," less "intellectual," more "sensitive," less "courageous," more "impulsive," less "serious-minded," more "subservient," or less "carnal." There may indeed be ways that females differ from males—other of course than the obvious anatomical and physiological ones—but which are innate and which are learned has now to be proved and can no longer be taken for granted.

It is hardly surprising that the image of woman could not have changed as it has without some corresponding alteration of the image of man. Changing a diaper or doing the dishes were standard cause for ridicule until women went to work outside the home in numbers. The fluctuating grounds for divorce have reflected woman's expanding sense of her rights, just as the increasing decisions for joint custody of children have reflected society's response to her assertion of those rights.

The self-portrait in the pages ahead of Frances Johnson, the photographer whose sense of fun matched her sense of the future, sums up the era before her. What it would all mean, and whether it could be called "progress," is something that perhaps only the lady with the crystal ball at the very start of these pages could tell.

164.   Smoking, drinking, and indecent exposure were thought to be beyond the pale. Noted photographer Frances B. Johnson mocks the female ideal in this self-portrait of 1896.

164

165.   Florodora Girls were synonymous
with wholesomeness and good looks. The
tableau of kneeling admirers suggests both
respectful homage to a feminine ideal and
the usual masculine appraisal of female
charms. But does woman have an essence
apart from either?

166.   These high steppers give the impression that they might have some symbolic hurdles in mind. Their expressions reflect the determination and exuberance that modern American women were bringing to the obstacle courses of their lives.

166

167.   The variety of heroines in silent films reflects America's groping toward a new image of woman in the first quarter of the twentieth century. Victorian sentimentality had not completely disappeared; as "America's Sweetheart," golden-curled Mary Pickford projected an enduring innocence.

168.   Theda Bara, the reigning "vampire," helped Americans acknowledge women's sexuality just before the onset of the roaring twenties. But she did so under the safe cover of an exoticism so removed from American realities that she hardly threatened conventional morality.

169.   Always refreshingly forthright and here clad in little but her underwear, Clara Bow succeeded in blending American innocence with an acceptable degree of naughtiness. A new era was starting in which the flapper was to become both lover and friend. Men would find it increasingly difficult to keep women within the old simplicities of wickedness and virtue. A changed image of woman began to inhabit Hollywood's dream world and, gradually, to transform the American woman herself.

170.   When this photograph was taken
of a Beauty Contest at Coney Island, the
amount of exposed female epidermis was
thought to be a measure of female emanci-
pation. Did the numbers around their
waists proclaim their anonymity or their
identity?

170

171.   These women were referred to as the Broom Brigade. Although we have no knowledge of what they were sighting over their brooms, we can be sure that a fair amount of suppressed hostility marked the lives of women between 1850 and 1930 as they dealt with autocratic husbands, tyrannical employers and condescending physicians. Women in work and play usually had to express their inner selves in some acceptably inoffensive way.

71

172.   The Chicago Junior League kicks up its heels in ladylike jubilation. Although their lives were in numbers of ways more secure than those of many women in the preceding pages, they too would come to know frustration and disappointment along with satisfaction and success. Whether milking the cow or carpooling the children, making box lunches or pounding a gavel, rejoicing in a good marriage, trying it again, or bypassing marriage altogether, the American female today is certainly more aware of what it is to be herself. While still in the process of sorting out her rights—social, legal, and emotional—she has learned from her predecessors the wisdom of tolerance, as well as of occasionally kicking up her heels.

Photo Credits

82.	Museum of the City of New York
83.	National Archives
84.	Library of Congress
85.	California Historical Society
86.	Constance Jacobs' personal collection
87.	Library of Congress
88.	Michigan State Archives
89.	Museum of the City of New York
90.	California Historical Society
91.	Museum of the City of New York
92.	Constance Jacobs' personal collection
93.	Idaho Historical Society
94.	Denver Public Library, Western History Collection
95.	Library of Congress
96.	Museum of the City of New York
97.	Nebraska Historical Society
98.	Library of Congress
99.	Constance Jacobs' personal collection
100.	Historical Society of New York City
101.	Adirondacks Museum
102.	University of Oregon
103.	Ohio Historical Society
104.	Museum of the City of New York
105.	Michigan State Archives
106.	Minnesota Historical Society
107.	Minnesota Historical Society
108.	Southern Oregon Historical Society
109.	Southern Oregon Historical Society
110.	State Historical Society of Wisconsin
111.	Oregon Historical Society
112.	Lane County Pioneer Museum, Oregon
113.	Kansas State Historical Society
114.	Nebraska State Historical Society
115.	Library of Congress
116.	Oregon Historical Society
117.	North Carolina Department of Archives and History
118.	National Archives
119.	North Carolina Department of Archives and History
120.	Southern Oregon Historical Society
121.	Lane County Pioneer Museum, Oregon
122.	Museum of the City of New York
123.	Museum of the City of New York
124.	Southern Oregon Historical Society
125.	Constance Jacobs' personal collection

126.	Colorado State Historical Society
127.	California Historical Society
128.	Minnesota Historical Society
129.	Library of Congress
130.	Constance Jacobs' personal collection
131.	Museum of the City of New York
132.	Museum of the City of New York
133.	Adirondacks Museum
134.	Library of Congress
135.	Constance Jacobs' personal collection
136–140.	Oregon Historical Society
141.	Constance Jacobs' personal collection
142.	Constance Jacobs' personal collection
143.	Southern Oregon Historical Society
144.	Vassar College Archives
145.	Kansas Historical Society
146.	Idaho Historical Society
147.	Constance Jacobs' personal collection
148.	Suzzallo Library Photo Collection, University of Washington, Photo by E. A. Hegg
149.	Library of Congress
150.	Minnesota Historical Society
151.	Museum of the City of New York
152.	Oregon Historical Society
153.	United Press International
154.	Library of Congress
155.	Oregon Historical Society
156.	National Archives
157.	National Archives
158.	Minnesota Historical Society
159.	State Historical Society of Wisconsin
160.	United Press International
161.	United Press International
162.	H. H. Bennett Studios
163.	University of Oregon
164.	Library of Congress
165.	Museum of the City of New York
166.	Library of Congress
167.	Museum of Modern Art, Film Collection
168.	Museum of Modern Art, Film Collection
169.	Museum of Modern Art, Film Collection
170.	United Press International
171.	Southern Oregon Historical Society
172.	Chicago Historical Society